Welcome to
Pathways: AXIS

This is my favorite time of the year for our church. This is the time where we ratchet up the intensity, bind closer together, and really focus on equipping, encouraging, and edifying one another toward experiencing the life God has envisioned for us. Over the next forty days, you will have the opportunity to participate in many personal and community activities designed to help you grow emotionally, spiritually, intellectually, physically, and societally.

These growth opportunities include: corporate worship gatherings, connexity events, service projects, Growth Groups, and this devotional journal written "by the community, for the community."

We will learn and worship as a whole church, and it is my prayer, and the prayer of the pastoral staff, that this will be an amazing time for your growth. A time where you will be able to look back in years to come and identify Pathways: AXIS as a transformational experience in your life.

In His Grip,
Pastor Mark

GOING DEEPER

Join the community and go deeper with this Bible study.

Breaking Ground:
What does it mean to be part of a community of faith?

The Dig:
Read 1 Corinthians 12:12-13.
What is the difference between *unity* and *uniformity*?

What are some different types of people groups who are in the church today?

What is the significance of baptism and the receiving of the same spirit? (v.13)

Read 1 Corinthians 12:14-17.
What is your contribution to the body of Christ?

Do you feel like your role is important and integral to the cause of Christ?

If you could do anything, as part of the body, what part would you be?

Read 1 Corinthians 12:18-26.
What other points does the body metaphor convey?

How does Paul counter our tendency toward pride in verses 18-26? How does this scripture help paint a clearer picture of Christian unity?

What is your response when another follower of Christ is hurting? What is a good example of the church sharing someone's suffering?

What is your gut feeling when another follower of Christ is honored? How can our church do a better job honoring one another?

Read 1 Corinthians 12:27-31.
Here Paul concludes his metaphor of the body with some specific roles in the church. What are other roles in the church that make it work? What role do you see yourself fulfilling?

Getting out of the hole:
Get involved! Start/Continue the journey to take ownership of God's design for you and His Body. Plug into the ministries at E3 to make, mature, and mobilize fully devoted followers of Christ. Pray about your gifting. Talk to a ministry leader about serving. Commit to a specific period of time to make sure you are being effective with your gifts and resources that God has entrusted to you.

Pathways: AXIS

UPCOMING EVENTS

- Serve Tallahassee
  9AM on 9/24

- Barbeque Cookoff
  330PM on 9/24

week 01 - community

Dear children, let's not merely say that we love each other; let us show the truth by our actions.
1 John 3:18

Community is a funny thing. A small group of caring friends can lighten the load of a sorrow, joking and laughter work best with two or more people sharing the joy, and an incorrigible strength can be felt in the midst of dozens or hundreds or thousands of people singing the praises of our God in one chorus.

But community can also be the source of heaps of frustration. Our deepest pain is often inflicted (directly or indirectly) by the ones closest to us. Some jokes can be at our own expense, leaving us alienated instead of connected. And even in a sea of voices, it can be all too easy to feel lost, alone, and unknown.

Most people have some sort of network of friends; the intrinsic desire for community is almost always pursued, in spite of any potential pain. But when we're asked to try to make new connections and share our thoughts and views with strangers, we often can only think of the risks involved in that level of vulnerability.

John, known as the Beloved Disciple, is clear in his letter, though. If we are truly going to live out loving others—which Jesus called the second greatest commandment, only behind loving God Himself—then we need to show our love in our actions. The statement is very active: do something to show your love for your brothers and sisters in Christ.

During this year's Pathways Journey, there are a number of things you can do to show your love. Join a Growth Group, commit to attending a Sunday gathering every week, read through this devotional, and most of all, share your experience. Love others by sharing yourself, opening up, and turning strangers into friends over the next six weeks. If you commit to growing in your relationships with God and with people, community can be more than just a "funny thing." Community can change your life.

Dan Durrenberger is the Pastor to Future Generations at Element3 Church where he leads E3Kids and E3 J-Hi. He and his wife, Lindsay, have been married for two years. He has recently found out that he is allergic to everything that is not awesome.

Pathways: AXIS

Journal your thoughts/response here:

Write words or
themes you need to
meditate on today. Schedule
four 5-minute time periods to
focus on these things.

day 01 - community

Earlier this week I received two separate pieces of devastating news. I was in my office, feeling alone, overwhelmed, and heartbroken. In the midst of tears, I updated my status on Facebook. I don't normally post every thought, feeling, or crisis. I thrive on real-life, close-up, personal relationships. No drive-by friendships for me! But at that moment, I posted a simple statement expressing my heartbreak.

Within minutes, I received several responses to my post - all encouraging words and promises to pray! By the end of that day, I had more than 20 comments, and between Carl and me, we received a dozen texts and calls with the same message of people making sure I was okay and offers of prayer. I have close relationships with some who responded, some are family, but many are people I am in community with at E3. Days later, poring over the comments again, I realized that some of the people who commented were new friends I'd met recently at a connexity event, a Sunday gathering, or while serving together at E3. All were people I had formed a connection with in some fashion. And that moment, the pain that I was experiencing was another connection point in our relationship.

I knew every comment was heartfelt, and that helped me get through the moments after my "crash." In my weakness when I felt like I didn't have the strength to lift my own prayers to God, others quickly stepped in and filled the gap, offering to help carry my burden- despite whatever was already on their plates.

I am now able to see that I would have survived that horrible time with or without the outpouring of love from each who commented, but the wound would have left a much deeper scar if my community hadn't provided that much needed care. How heavy the load would have been without those who shared the weight - at least 20 times heavier!

Lori Green is on staff at E3 and serves on many of E3's ministry teams, including the Musical Worship Team. Married to the love of her life, Carl, she has four amazing kids, ages 10 - 27. She enjoys singing and spending time with friends.

Pathways: AXIS

Journal your thoughts/response here:

Write words or themes you need to meditate on today. Schedule four 5-minute time periods to focus on these things.

day 02 - community

Let us think of ways to motivate one another to acts of love and good works. And let us not neglect our meeting together, as some people do, but encourage one another, especially now that the day of his return is drawing near.
Hebrews 10:24-25

A question I've heard asked a lot in my travels is why does E3 emphasize community? What's the point? I come on Sunday, I sing, I take what the message says and try to live it out as best I can. Isn't that enough?

The truth is that it's not enough. This passage in Hebrews helps shed further light on why we should be in community. God wants us to walk together to motivate each other to acts of love and good works. He wants us to come together and encourage one another. Only through all parts of the body working together can the love of Jesus Christ be fully expressed and the Great Commission be fulfilled. In order for us to work together, we must spend time with each other.

On a Sunday at E3, it's only possible to have a small amount of personal interaction with others. My hope is that each of you will get involved with a Growth Group and stay involved in it through Pathways and beyond. In the intimacy of each other's homes, we have the opportunity to build friendships, learn more about what God is calling us to, and spend time in laughter (which is what most GGs I've been a part of do).

In my own life, I've been fortunate to cultivate a group of people with whom I live, eat, work, and hang out on the weekends. We laugh together, we cry together, we rejoice in good times, and we mourn in others. Knowing that there is a group of people who have my back, and that I have theirs, as we push towards the cross together, makes walking this earth that much better.

I hope that you will spend time investing in finding biblical community, and that through this journey, you will begin walking a path with other people that will echo throughout eternity.

Trace Armstrong is the Director of Branding and Communications and can occasionally be seen foraying into Worship Arts where he leads musical worship. If you wish to approach him in conversation, he enjoys barbecue, movies, music, vinyl LPs, guitars, football, hockey (GO CAPS!!!), hardwood floors, things that are shiny, and he is highly allergic to shrimp.

Pathways: AXIS

Journal your thoughts/response here:

Write words or
themes you need to
meditate on today. Schedule
four 5-minute time periods to
focus on these things.

day 03 - community

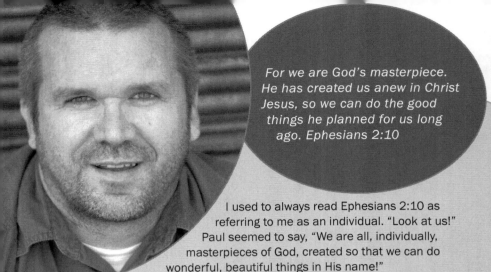

> *For we are God's masterpiece. He has created us anew in Christ Jesus, so we can do the good things he planned for us long ago. Ephesians 2:10*

I used to always read Ephesians 2:10 as referring to me as an individual. "Look at us!" Paul seemed to say, "We are all, individually, masterpieces of God, created so that we can do wonderful, beautiful things in His name!"

While there is definitely a personal dynamic to this quote, for the past year or so I've come to realize that there is another dimension to "God's Art." You see, the book of Ephesians is largely about the Church: this beautiful coming-together of Jews and Gentiles, all under the banner of Jesus Christ. So when Paul says, "we are God's masterpiece," Paul could also be referring to the fact that the masterpiece—this diverse, sometimes-messy group of people following Jesus—is actually the Church as a body.

God not only sees us as individual masterpieces, He sees our efforts to live in community—our efforts to reconcile, to understand our differences, to bear each other's burdens—all as beautiful pieces of a mosaic, one that He is putting together.

This challenges me when I look around me. Sometimes I have to own up to the fact that I prefer people who often look like me, think like me, and see the world the way I do. Unfortunately, that's not the reality of the Church. In fact, the body that God created brought people together across ethnic, political, and economic lines.

The more we embrace, work through, and even celebrate our differences, the more we resemble the diverse group of people in the early church. While occasionally drifting back to our communal "safety zones" is normal, maybe today you can pause and think about your circles: do they look like the mosaic masterpiece that God envisioned, or do they resemble a painting that has been done using only one or two colors?

Eric Case is the Pastor of Musical Worship at E3. He is "Shana's husband," and father to Emily and Levi. He loves learning and teaching and playing "rock 'n roll."

Pathways: AXIS

Journal your thoughts/response here:

Write words or
themes you need to
meditate on today. Schedule
four 5-minute time periods to
focus on these things.

day 04 - community

Life together is brilliant... illuminating. I never cease to be amazed at the insights of the people around me. I never cease to be humbled by the gifts and resources that others possess and freely wield to bring the spiritual kingdom of God abruptly into the physical world.

Hands revealing hearts that have been transformed. Mouths pouring balm onto gaping wounds unhealed by the wisdom of the world, yet soothed and safeguarded by the words of life that true followers ooze through their speech and behavior. Minds that choose to give their fellow humans second chances as acts of worship to their longsuffering and ever-loving Creator. Faces that reflect (especially in the darkest times) the glorious light of their Savior with smiles that beckon like an open door to unalterable peace.

And yes, there is chafing - division and conflict and strife at times. But there is more than enough grace for those things if we will let Him soften our hearts. Grace changes everything. Grace changes me if I dare encounter it. It sets me free to forgive and to love without fear of pain. Grace kills pain. It moves to destroy pain with all the skill of a predator and the heart of a healer. Grace in action killed Christ and then raised Him from the dead. This is the abnormal life of the miraculous... the story of living in grace.

Grace breathes fire, but only to burn away the disease of selfishness inside us. It cauterizes the brokenness of our depravity and stops the flow to the black hole of self. It burns away the dross of our depravity and lets us shine with the light of God's love. Grace grows in the expression of our lives as we understand who we are compared to who God is, then believe in His deadly love for us that defines our worth, and finally, live as conduits of His lavish love.

We are the people of second chances. We are the people of grace. Grow in it. Abound in it. Share it.

Dan Meyer is married to Rene' and they have 3 amazing children - Jael, Elijah and Aria - all born in June. He loves to spend time exploring and engaging the great outdoors.

Pathways: AXIS

Journal your thoughts/response here:

Write words or themes you need to meditate on today. Schedule four 5-minute time periods to focus on these things.

day 05 - community

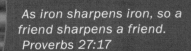

> As iron sharpens iron, so a
> friend sharpens a friend.
> Proverbs 27:17

Eight years ago, before E3 was born, I was having a passionate discussion with Lori Green (who is now my Administrative Assistant and leads Inward and Outward Connexity at E3) over the word, connexity. Although she whole-heartedly believed in the importance of connecting people with community, she did not agree with using a word that was not in the dictionary (a burden I do not carry). To help her through this Webster-induced bondage, I may have implied that it was going to be in next year's dictionary, so there really wasn't any conflict at all. At that she yielded and embraced the word connexity ("embraced" may be overstated a tad bit).

Since that time, every year when the new updated dictionaries come out, I am informed by my lovely assistant that connexity is still not in there. At that, I reply, "I heard it is going to be in next year's dictionary." Does it matter if connexity is in the dictionary? I don't think it matters to God what we call it, as long as His people are connecting in biblical community. Actively being in community is the heart of our faith. Our God is a triune God, who exists in perfect community as the Father, Son, and Holy Spirit. His desire for community with His creation, lead Him to break perfect fellowship in order to give us the opportunity to have a right relationship with Him and others. Every command, story, and teaching, given by God to us in His word, is given to help us experience an extraordinary life defined by this right relationship with God and people.

Mark Foreman, in his book Wholly Jesus, encompasses the holistic nature of connexity by saying, "We [the Church] should be in motion toward restoring people as bio-psycho-socio-spiritual beings while always restoring their relationship with God through forgiveness in Christ." Connexity is the motion toward that restoration. Let us continue moving forward.

Hey Lori! I hear CONNEXITY is going to be in the 2012 dictionary.

Pastor Mark McNees is the Lead and founding pastor of Element3 Church. When he is not teaching, writing, meeting, or vision casting at E3 he doubles for Governor Rick Scott in hostile situations.

Pathways: AXIS

Journal your thoughts/response here:

Write words or themes you need to meditate on today. Schedule four 5-minute time periods to focus on these things.

day 06 - community

Then Jesus said, "Come to me, all of you who are weary and carry heavy burdens, and I will give you rest." Matthew 11:28

Growing up in the church, I always thought the Sabbath was Sunday, and on Sundays we all went to church, and, of course, all businesses were closed. It was a time of rest if for no other reason than because there was nothing else to do.

Well, as I got older, I learned that the Sabbath was not technically Sunday, and slowly but surely, almost every business started opening on Sunday. But the purpose of the Sabbath never changed; a day dedicated to God and His holiness and a time of rest for us. With today's hectic pace and lifestyles, I believe our need for a Sabbath is greater than ever. In fact, I don't think one day is enough.

My wife and I were discussing this, and the words of Jesus in Matthew 11:28 came to mind. We realized that in these words Jesus was saying that He is our Sabbath. He is where we go for rest and strength. He is who we are dedicated to. He is what is to be kept holy.

Jesus is our Sabbath. We go to him when we are weary or burdened, and in Him we find rest. If that is true, then it brings a whole new insight into Jesus' statement about the Sabbath.

Mark 2:27 reads, Then Jesus said to them, "The Sabbath was made to meet the needs of people, and not people to meet the requirements of the Sabbath."

Wow. I find great comfort in these words. Jesus was made to meet my needs. Not my petty needs, but my deeper ones. The need for a savior. The need to be brought back into communion with God. The need to be made whole once again, and to find peace and rest in the holiness of our God. Remember this the next time you are burdened, or weary, or in need of rest, or searching for holiness. Jesus is our Sabbath.

Charlie Vanture is a guitar-slinging lawyer and is 1/3 of the Sarah Mac Band. Some think he practices playing guitar more than practicing law.

Pathways: AXIS

Journal your thoughts/response here:

Write words or
themes you need to
meditate on today. Schedule
four 5-minute time periods to
focus on these things.

day 07 - sabbath

GOING DEEPER

Join the community and go deeper with this Bible study.

Breaking Ground:

What first comes to mind when you hear the word, "worship?" Is it a place? Time? Activity?

The Dig:

Read John 4:21-26.
What does this scripture tell us about worship?

What does "worship in spirit and truth" mean?

How is "worship in spirit and truth" lived out?

What is the significance of Jesus' original proclamation, about Him being the Messiah, Samaritan woman?

Read Matthew 18:20.
How does this verse impact your view on location-based worship?

Read Matthew 12:6 and John 2:19-22.
According to Jesus, what/who is the destination of our worship?

What does the realization of Jesus being the Temple mean to you in your pursuit of being devoted follower of Christ?

Getting out of the hole:

Worship happens in the presence of Jesus and is not bound to a location. Get out and God in a unique and new place this week. Make a plan to do this as an individual AND with a group of friends.

Pathways: AXIS

Journal your thoughts/response here:

week 02 - worship

On the bus to Kingston, NY, I got the call. My housing plans had fallen through; I was hours from arriving with nowhere to stay. I would be homeless in my hometown. And yet, I wasn't worried. I prayed and felt I should call my home church in NY. A volunteer overheard the call and offered to let me stay with her family. She'd never met me before and only volunteered there once a week. Praise God! I stayed in their peaceful home and had a wonderful time.

The point though, was my response to the "bad news." It was more than the prayer and hearing from God. It was peace. A friend asked why I was so peaceful in that moment, knowing that I've struggled with worry. The answer was simple. I had been reading God's word and spending time with Him each day.

This past year, wanting more of the Lord's direction, peace, and presence in my life, I challenged myself to read the Bible and pray for His guidance each morning. It wasn't perfectly done, but I regularly studied, prayed, and surrendered myself to God's direction. Some mornings were just short passages and a dedication, while others were very engrossing and prayerful. I could feel the Lord changing my thoughts and behavior. I knew I was gaining a personal, tangible grasp of the Lord, my relationship with Him, and practical ways we can honor Him in our daily lives. Scriptures were no longer just on the page, screen, or radio. They were written on my heart. When my housing plans fell through, I wasn't worried because of the truth and peace inside of me. I knew God would make a way, and He did. Our response to life's challenges is subject to our foundation in Him.

I have much to learn in my practice of prayer and study, but I definitely know it's making a difference. Let's routinely study God's tangible word together and collectively pray for His guidance. It's more than an investment of our time. It's a high calling. It's personal, daily, life-changing worship. And it's totally worth it.

Jamie Kassler recently graduated from the College of Motion Picture Arts at FSU with a focus in directing and seeks to impact the world through the power of film.

Pathways: AXIS

Journal your thoughts/response here:

Write words or themes you need to meditate on today. Schedule four 5-minute time periods to focus on these things.

day 08 - worship

If you had asked me one or more years ago what I thought of when I heard the word "worship," you most likely would have had one of two reactions. You either would have giggled to yourself and thought I was attempting to play the role of a standup comedian, or you would have wondered where in the world I was from and how I escaped. My response would have been along the lines of worship being Thursday morning chapel services at my school, requiring me to wear a dress or skirt and dress shoes; or Sunday morning youth group followed by a grueling hour and a half lecture in the auditorium.

It was not until I found E3 one year ago that the light turned on, and I realized worshiping God was not supposed to be a chore, but a time of joy and a connection straight to the throne of Jesus. I realized at that time that to get the full benefit of worship you must have a relationship with Christ. It is similar to dieting - you can work out for hours a day, but if you don't eat healthy, you will not reap the full benefit.

Even after realizing I had things all wrong, worship through music still was uncomfortable. Sure, E3 sang songs that were easier to enjoy and often left me feeling alive rather than half asleep and dreading the next one, but it was still slightly uncomfortable for me. I have learned that Jesus never promised us that things would be simple, but sometimes it is about stepping outside of your comfort zone, realizing God is on your side, thanking Him, and offering praises to Him for that simple fact.

I think of the song we often sing, "...and if our God is with us, then what could stand against?" It is true!! God is on our side, and He has our back. It is our duty as followers of Him to thank Him for this and show our gratitude through worship. If we are worshiping from our hearts, that peace and excitement radiates from us for others who are skeptical (like I was), and they will see the pure happiness that abounds from worship with our Lord and Savior.

Rebecca White has been married for seven years and has been blessed with four beautiful babies: Rachael Kinsey, Ramsey Kendall II, Rayna Kimber, and Roman Kade.

Pathways: AXIS

Journal your thoughts/response here:

Write words or themes you need to meditate on today. Schedule four 5-minute time periods to focus on these things.

day 09 - worship

God-fearing Gentiles"... Recently, I realized how big of a deal it was when Paul said those words. Preaching to Israel was normal, but speaking to Gentiles was still new, and calling them God-fearing was a strong statement. These people were the foreign and the unclean, not the chosen people of God. Faith in Him was not for them, but all that changed with the death and resurrection of Jesus.

Another translation says, "...you Gentiles who worship God." I get this picture in my head of Israelites and Gentiles singing together, their voices mixing into one without the separation of "the chosen" and "the unclean."

Recently, Dan Meyer asked our students what worship meant to them. Hannah Wilkes said, "It [worship] makes everyone equal. It doesn't matter if you're a pastor or a drug addict." I like that idea. All of us, those far from God or those close to Him, are the same when it comes to true worship. This is what was happening with Paul, and it happens in our culture today.

The American church has a reputation of treating people like the Israelites treated the Gentiles. Even our church culture would think of some as unclean or dirty sinners. But, have you ever listened on a Sunday morning to the sound of everyone singing together? I love how it sounds when the instruments pull back and everyone is making one voice. Like Hannah said, we are all one - all of us are worshiping our Creator, the one who says we are all valuable to Him.

Worshiping God is not only for one special group. Whether it is music or how we live our lives, all of us who call ourselves followers of Christ are brought together. That is one of the things about E3 that is so wonderful. We belong to a community that strives to treat all of God's creations the same. E3 realizes we are all Gentiles that God has said are precious to Him. "This is our story; this is our song, praising our Savior all the day long."

Ward Hughey has been at part of E3 for almost 7 years. He was raised in small town USA (Madison, FL) and came to Tallahassee in 2003 to attend FSU. He has a degree in psychology, and lives for relationship, working with teenagers, and music.

Pathways: AXIS

Journal your thoughts/response here:

Write words or themes you need to meditate on today. Schedule four 5-minute time periods to focus on these things.

day 10 - worship

I have always disliked my name. When I was a little girl, I did not like it because no one said it correctly-they always left out the "r" calling me "Maaatha." As I grew older and learned more about the people in the Bible, I liked it even less because I realized that Martha was too busy and didn't have time to sit at Jesus' feet like Mary. And when people started saying that I was appropriately named, and, "You really are a Martha," I truly began to loathe my name. Okay, so maybe I don't know how to "be still" very well.

Late one afternoon in Haiti, I was sitting still waiting for everyone to finish their work and climb into the truck to go home. Next to me sat a little boy named Snyder. He was snuggled beside me, and we were just sitting together as the sun was setting into the ocean just beyond the garbage dump and the salt flats of Jubilee Blanc. Snyder didn't know English, and I didn't speak much Creole, so we really couldn't talk to each other. He could not tell me anything nor could he ask me for anything, but this child was content to just "be" with me. All he wanted was to be close to me, to feel my arm securely around him, and to somehow know he was special to me.

Oh, how I long to be like Snyder. I want to be content to just sit and be still with my heavenly Father, my Papa. I want to let Him love on me, and I want to snuggle up close to Him, quiet and still. Why do I always feel like I have to be talking to Him about some situation or asking Him to give me something? Snyder, a seven year old boy in Haiti, taught me a very important lesson that day. There are times when I need to be still and know that He is God, content with a quiet cuddle. Yes, I can worship even when I am not doing a thing or saying a word.

Martha Hanna is a wife to Michael; a mama to Katie, Will, and Brayton; a mother-in-law to Cody; a home-school teacher; a nursing instructor; a therapeutic horseback-riding instructor; and a lover of missions to both Haiti and Guatemala.

Pathways: AXIS

Journal your thoughts/response here:

Write words or themes you need to meditate on today. Schedule four 5-minute time periods to focus on these things.

day 11 - worship

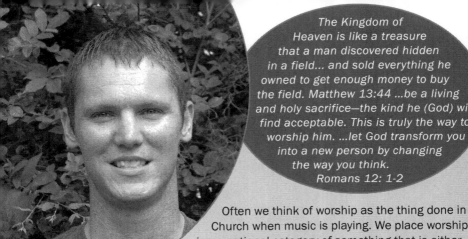

The Kingdom of Heaven is like a treasure that a man discovered hidden in a field... and sold everything he owned to get enough money to buy the field. Matthew 13:44 ...be a living and holy sacrifice—the kind he (God) will find acceptable. This is truly the way to worship him. ...let God transform you into a new person by changing the way you think.
Romans 12: 1-2

Often we think of worship as the thing done in Church when music is playing. We place worship in an optional category of something that is either done or not done. But worship is something performed at all times by all people. Not optional, but inherent to human experience. More than that, worship is tied to what we believe about things. Worship, in essence, is anytime belief becomes action.

What happens in this story from Matthew is actually a profound act of worship. Value is ascribed to the field because of what is in it, and thus sacrifices are made. Money is spent... a field is purchased... because the field contained something that transformed belief.

So worship is action that comes from beliefs. Beliefs come from the heart. We mistakenly think they are of the mind - constructed of reasons - but belief is closer to emotion. It exists to preserve the reality of things we love. Think of someone who just heard about a loved one's death. Often there is a struggle to accept this news. Science tells us we do it involuntarily when we want to preserve a needed reality. I once saw a video where a group of Wall Street brokers were asked if they thought the US economy could ever collapse. They answered without hesitation, "That will never happen." A few even said, "Impossible." When asked for their economic reasoning, they all faltered to supply a quick answer. Why? Because what we love determines our beliefs. Their hearts confessed what they needed to be true.

Love determines belief. Belief transforms actions. Actions = worship.

We are the ones called to make a difference. What is our "field of treasure"? The thing so valuable we give all for it. The thing our hearts immediately confess. Or perhaps our hearts are revealing things of worship we dare not admit? All life is sacrificed for something. What is yours?

Josh Waite is a covenanted owner at E3. He enjoys connecting people to community and participating in worship arts.

Pathways: AXIS

Journal your thoughts/response here:

Write words or themes you need to meditate on today. Schedule four 5-minute time periods to focus on these things.

day 12 - worship

I love this story because it reminds me that through worship comes victory! Often, in the Bible, God uses worship instead of armies and tactical might to win battles. God wants me to remember to worship Him continually throughout the day, no matter what is happening. He wants me to remember that, "The Lord himself will fight for you. Just stay calm." (Exodus 14:14)

He wants me to worship Him throughout the day with songs and by keeping my mind on Him and His truth. Listening to music which reminds me of Him, reading something from the Bible each day, and writing out an encouraging verse on an index card to keep with me, are ways that help me to focus on God and to remember that He will fight my battles for me!

God is my perfect parent! He never gets tired of me, He never forgets me, and He never tries to get rid of me by saying, "Fight your own battles!" Instead, He encourages me, in the toughest times, to find something to be thankful for, something to praise Him for, and my praise becomes daily, living worship to Him. Living in a continual attitude of praise and thanksgiving for God's mercy which endures forever does not guarantee a life free of problems, sadness, and disappointment. It does guarantee that God will fight for me. Instead of thinking about the negative things which have happened to me, I choose to thank God for the many things which He has not let happen to me!

Judy Abbott loves baking for people and dogs!

Pathways: AXIS

Journal your thoughts/response here:

Write words or themes you need to meditate on today. Schedule four 5-minute time periods to focus on these things.

day 13 - worship

Growing up, my mother said to me on many occasions, "You'd better change your attitude, young lady." I would change my behavior but considered my attitude off limits. The way I think about the world impacts how I react to it and interact with others. God wants me to know the world through His perspective. This amazing gift allows me to live in His good, pleasing and perfect will. Sign me up! Well, like all good things... I have to dedicate the time.

Practical Exercise: Let's print out a copy of our calendars for last Thursday. Now, write on that printout all the other activities for that day that you did not record. Be as detailed as possible. Got up, walked the dog, took a shower...etc. Does it seem full to you?

Our way of everyday life does not encourage a Sabbath for our minds, yet scripture tells us this is necessary to be in line with God's perfect plan for our lives. To allow God to change the WAY I think, I have to regularly give my mind a rest from the world. Scripture guides us all; my time of mental rest makes that guidance specific to me.

So... back to the calendar. Everyone is different; what will work best for you? What does it take to plug in to God and unplug from everything else? Fifteen minutes three times a day and an occasional day at the beach? I seem to need bigger blocks of time to allow me to unplug and realign my focus - maybe a weekend each month. Where are the times I can say "no" to my schedule and "yes" to God?

Our daily obligations can be a parasite to our connection with our Father. To live abundantly and as a blessing to the world around us, we must continually detox our minds from this world and refocus on the will of God. I'm going to pen in some regular Sabbath time appointments on my schedule. I need to change my attitude, and this time I want to!

Mary Coffee is a mountain girl living in a beach community. She loves creating, researching, planning and spending time talking and laughing with friends. She is currently focusing on detoxing her body, mind and house.

Pathways: AXIS

Journal your thoughts/response here:

Write words or themes you need to meditate on today. Schedule four 5-minute time periods to focus on these things.

day 14 - sabbath

GOING DEEPER

Join the community and go deeper with this Bible study.

Breaking Ground:

What is your favorite thing about mud?

The Dig:

Read John 9.

How do you feel when you think about outreach/evangelism?

What was the presupposition of the disciples' question to Jesus? (v.1)

What does Jesus' answer tell us about physical brokenness? (v.3-5)

How does this translate into your own pain and brokenness?

What is the "task" Jesus is speaking about? (v.3)

Why were the religious leaders so angry? (v.16)

Why did Jesus keep healing people on the Sabbath if he knew it angered the religious leaders so much?

What are your thoughts about how the blind man responded to the religious leaders?

Why do you think the parents responded how they did?

What do you think the religious rulers' real motives were behind their anger?

Who had a better view of God, the religious rulers or the blind man?

What does this tell us about being an expert?

Getting out of the hole:

Your story is important. This week, look for opportunities to share it. Ask God to give you an opportunity to worship Him by sharing the story of His faithfulness to you with someone who is far from Him.

Pathways: AXIS

UPCOMING EVENTS

• Serve Tallahassee
  9AM on 10/8

week 03 - outreach

Love, by our Lord Jesus' standards, is the greatest decision a person can make. He even goes so far as to state in His word that without love there is no meaning to anything we pursue in this life. Having said this, I believe that love is the driving factor behind outreach, as well as obedience and sacrifice. God the Father sacrificed His only son, and Jesus chose to obey so that we could be reconciled to them and our relationship restored. The decision of reconciliation is given to all mankind, but not all are able to see the light, and even those that do will not always choose it. Our job as followers of Christ is to be a beacon of light to the lost souls in this dark world.

In 2004, I entered a program for women called the Walter Hoving Home, which is a women's rehabilitation home. They reach out to all types of women from all walks of life that are in need of a change. After the women enter the home they are nurtured and given resources to help them build a relationship with their Savior. They are also given chances to be involved in the ministry in a number of ways; the one I chose was The Outreach Department.

God placed the desire in my heart to help continue the work that he started, reaching out to a hurting world with compassion and sincerity. Love, obedience, and sacrifice, in my opinion, are some of the attributes necessary when reaching out into a hurting world. It is not always easy to follow God's guidance, especially when it takes sacrifice; but in the end, if we truly love Him, we will care for those he cares for and follow His direction, not condemning others, but loving them just as Christ would.

Krista Campos has a passion for outreach ministry because of the love her God has for her and the compassion He has given her for His creation.

Pathways: AXIS

Journal your thoughts/response here:

Write words or
themes you need to
meditate on today. Schedule
four 5-minute time periods to
focus on these things.

day 15 - outreach

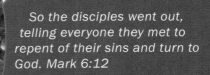

So the disciples went out, telling everyone they met to repent of their sins and turn to God. Mark 6:12

Bold love will make a difference for God's kingdom. A gift, a hug, or investing time are ways that I express love to others around me, but I get angry at myself when I simply love someone. Not because they don't show me love back, but because I forget to express love to them in its purest form.

What Jesus did for us on the cross - grace - can't be cheapened with mere action. Don't get me wrong. Expressing love through action is critical to our walk with Christ. Faith without action is indeed dead; it's an example of Christ's love.

How can those who are lost hear if they do not listen? And how can they listen if we who know of salvation in Christ do not tell them? Jesus cannot be found in a new electric guitar or an expensive dinner. Jesus is fully realized in hearing about Jesus, not worldly love. He does not reincarnate Himself in an item or a belief system. If we believe in God's Word - the Word that God Himself breathed into life - then how can we possibly believe that someone will find salvation in Jesus if what He did for us is not shared?

In Mark 6:1-6, Jesus was rejected by His home-town after warning and teaching them His truth, and He was amazed at their unbelief. Later, in verse 11, Jesus instructs His disciples (that also means us) that they are to walk away from anyone who rejects the good news, and to "abandon those people to their fate." Some people will not listen, but some people will listen. If you are a Christ-follower, and you desire to live for Christ's calling, then that means you need to go out into your community and don't wait for an opportunity, but make an opportunity to share with someone Christ's redeeming love. Bold love will make a difference for God's kingdom. Let's share the truth in love.

Eric Rivera is 23 years old, the fourth of six kids, and from Miami, FL. He will be graduating in December of 2011 from FSU in Business Management. He has no idea where he will be in January of 2012, but he's okay with that because God has a plan.

Pathways: AXIS

Journal your thoughts/response here:

Write words or themes you need to meditate on today. Schedule four 5-minute time periods to focus on these things.

day 16 - outreach

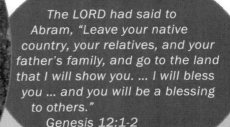

The LORD had said to Abram, "Leave your native country, your relatives, and your father's family, and go to the land that I will show you. ... I will bless you ... and you will be a blessing to others."
Genesis 12:1-2

Melanie and I worked a week with a short-term mission team in Guatemala in 2004. Seemingly out of nowhere, I felt a strong leading to leave my law firm and move our family to Panajachel to start an unconventional ministry there. It seemed crazy and was scary. There were plenty of tears as we considered what God was calling us to.

Several months later I returned to Guatemala, secretly hoping that God (or someone) would show us that I had misunderstood and that we did not need to go. Returning to Guate City for lost luggage, we visited a little mission church where a young seminarian preached in Spanish. As the music played at the start of the service, I begged God for direction and clarity. My translator's eyes moistened as the preacher began the scripture reading, "God had said to Abram, leave ... others." I heard, in my spirit, "Do you believe this?" It was the most direct God-message I'd ever received. I'm convinced we would have lost our nerve had it not been so direct. True to the promise, we've been blessed and we've been a blessing. We praise God for that.

I've learned this: God will provide direction and confirmation for outreach that we're intended to do. Many times our human nature is to "rationalize away" and not do tasks or make changes that we might be called to. Most often, such tasks or changes require that we, like Abram, leave what, or who, might be comfortable or that holds us back. Here's to bold leaving!

Lloyd and Melanie Monroe were in the initial E3 Stage classes, founded Porch de Salomon and have served as full-time volunteers in Guatemala since 2005.

Pathways: AXIS

Journal your thoughts/response here:

Write words or themes you need to meditate on today. Schedule four 5-minute time periods to focus on these things.

day 17 - outreach

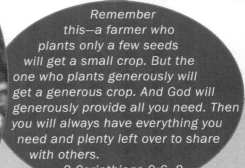

To me, outreach is the part of witnessing where the rubber meets the road. What constitutes a witness? Is it someone who goes out on the street witnessing to individuals or open-air preaching? Yes, that's one form. Is it talking to friends and family about salvation? Yes, that's another. But how do we really impact the community? I believe it is by being who we are in Christ and doing what He told us to do. It is "being the tangible hand of Christ." (Matt 25:35-40)

A minister named Dr. Henry Gruver was called to walk cities and pray, led by the Holy Spirit, witnessing to those God put in his path. While walking and praying one night he was led to a man who was hostile toward God. The man took him to where he was living with his wife and children - in an attic. They had no food. That is why he was angry at God. Dr. Gruver took the man grocery shopping. They all believed in Christ that night.

If we want their souls to be filled with the love of God, we first have to fill their stomachs with the provision of God. Pastor Mark said once, "Wouldn't it be amazing if when a politician proposed a new food program for the hungry, people would scratch their heads and wonder, Why? Since there are no hungry people because the church has already taken care of it?" I agree. I would add, "Wouldn't it be amazing if every church in America would take a plot of land and grow a community garden to feed the church and the poor in the community?"

We could feed not only ourselves, but the poor as well and what we save on food bills could go back into the ministry of the church, and God would multiply it all! It's something to seriously consider. What do you think? How could you help?

Bryan Scott is a returning student at TCC who will then transfer to FSU for Engineering. He is divorced with three children, Kenny (23), Aaron (22), and Bryana (15).

Pathways: AXIS

Journal your thoughts/response here:

Write words or
themes you need to
meditate on today. Schedule
four 5-minute time periods to
focus on these things.

day 18 - outreach

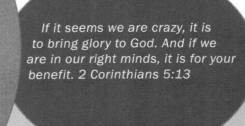

If it seems we are crazy, it is to bring glory to God. And if we are in our right minds, it is for your benefit. 2 Corinthians 5:13

He smiled at me with a grin as wide as a quarter moon from his dark-skinned face. "Are you crazy?" he asked. Jean Baptiste had just asked the very question my wife Martha and I had often asked ourselves in the past year and a half. It caught me off guard.

Jean and his friends were with me, kicking a soccer ball and talking about life here in the slums of Haiti. The sunset was amazing over the salt flats. I had just commented on how beautiful it was here. "Am I crazy?" The terrain here was exactly as I pictured the moon to be like: barren, dusty and covered with small rocks. There is no life here except that which our group had planted. The wind blows the salt-laced dirt into your eyes and mouth, covering you with a fine layer of dust, which mixes with your sweat and never goes away. The boys stared at me waiting for an answer.

Immediately after the earthquake in Haiti, Martha jumped onto an airplane to go help. Here we were a year and a half later, standing in a part of Haiti even the UN wouldn't go into, building housing and a school, teaching marketable art and medical skills, and building community with our Haitian friends. "Am I crazy?"

How silly it must have seemed to them that these "Blancs" would come here to a garbage dump and call it *beautiful*. "You make it beautiful," I said to them. "Without you, this is just a dump. You bring joy, love, and enthusiasm for Christ here to the clinic and the school. We are learning from each other and are becoming a community, and that is a beautiful thing!" We shared a common bond in Christ. White, black, blessed with resources or poor, we met at a common place in our hearts and encouraged each other in our journey with Christ. As we reach out locally and globally, we cannot truly have a tangible impact until we are united by Christ and his beauty.

"He makes beautiful things out of the dust. He makes beautiful things out of us." - Gungor

Michael Hanna is a husband to Martha, a daddy to Katie, Will, and Brayton, a father-in-law to Cody, a physical therapist, Global Outreach Leader, and frequent traveler to Guatemala and Haiti.

Pathways: AXIS

Journal your thoughts/response here:

Write words or themes you need to meditate on today. Schedule four 5-minute time periods to focus on these things.

day 19 - outreach

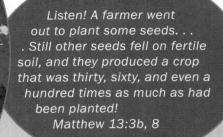

Listen! A farmer went out to plant some seeds. . . . Still other seeds fell on fertile soil, and they produced a crop that was thirty, sixty, and even a hundred times as much as had been planted!
Matthew 13:3b, 8

Reaching out to others with the Gospel of Christ has always been one of my major weaknesses. Being naturally quiet and reserved, the more traditional door-to-door handing people Bible tracts and sharing the gospel form of witnessing wasn't my style. Furthermore, when asked or given the opportunity to partake in such activities, I would often decline.

Over the past few years, I have learned that it is not about going door-to-door and sharing the gospel outright. Instead, we must build relationships with the people God brings into our lives, gently pulling the weeds until their hearts are ready to be introduced to Christ (if we even get to be the one to do that; it can sometimes take the work of many farmers for a seed to sprout). Relational right, as those who have attended E3 for any length of time have undoubtedly heard, is key for building and fortifying the lives of those entrusted to us. It allows us to speak into the deeper aspects of their lives, planting seeds that will help them reach their potential.

"That's great, but I'm the only one who has the relational right to speak into _____'s life about living for Christ, and they're not interested in coming to church with me. What do I do now?" It will likely take significant time for a person's heart to be willing to accept Christ. In the meantime, turn to those who speak into yours. Ask them for guidance, suggestions and prayer, for both you and the other person. You are not alone when it comes to reaching out to the world around us; the local church community is behind you in your pursuit to reach out to others.

What seeds has God entrusted you to sow?

Father, thank you for providing us with the knowledge, tools, and support we need to reach out to the lost and hurting world around us. Give us the boldness to step out, build relationships, and sow seeds into the lives you have entrusted us with. In the name of Jesus, Amen.

Virginia Summerell has attended E3 since 2008. She can be found serving coffee most Sunday's before the 11AM gathering and is currently pursuing a master's degree in human services.

Pathways: AXIS

Journal your thoughts/response here:

Write words or themes you need to meditate on today. Schedule four 5-minute time periods to focus on these things.

day 20 - outreach

Be still before the Lord and wait patiently for Him. Psalm 37:7

"I just want to do something." "I feel so helpless." These are common reactions when people are confronted with circumstances beyond their control such as an illness, death, or other loss. However, these times may be a call for us to quit struggling and rest in Christ. Our culture has taught us that if we are experiencing crisis, we must not be trying hard enough, or not trying the right solution. If you don't believe me, just browse the self-help section of any bookstore for evidence of this. Christ's response is that we need to quit trying and rest in Him.

There can be tremendous fear in admitting that you are not in control of a situation. But this is what God asks us to do. That is the essence of faith in God. I struggle with this at times. When things go wrong, I usually ask God, "What have I done to deserve this?" Of course, sometimes my problems are the result of my own actions, but God's usual reply in times of trouble is, "Be still. You are not in control. I AM."

This can seem scary, but when it comes down to it, God is offering us what we need in times of trouble – a rest. He wants us to know that we don't need to try to earn His love or His gifts, just like your kids do not need to earn the love or gifts you give them. It is your pleasure to provide for them, just as God receives pleasure in providing good things for us (Matthew 7:11). This is what resting in Him teaches us.

Take some time to enjoy God's rest. The Biblical concept of the Sabbath is to take one day a week to rest from your work and reflect on who is the true source of your provision. Take some time to set aside your efforts and rest in Christ. Do something that you enjoy and that allows you to focus on what God has done for you. See if this changes your perspective about who really controls your future.

Louie Serna is married to Suzie Serna and is the dad of Christian (13) and Joy (9). He finds that time in nature near the water helps him feel closer to God. When it comes to resting, he doesn't always practice what he preaches.

Pathways: AXIS

Journal your thoughts/response here:

Write words or themes you need to meditate on today. Schedule four 5-minute time periods to focus on these things.

day 21 - sabbath

GOING DEEPER

Join the community and go deeper with this Bible study.

Breaking Ground:
Who was your biggest champion growing up?

The Dig:
Read Galatians 6:1-10.

How do verses 1-2 show a healthy way of helping someone live out the vision God has for their life?

What should be the goal when a brother or sister in Christ stumbles?

How have you seen this handled in the past?

What are some failures that the church seems to have difficulty with in pursuing restoration?

Why is this?

What other scriptures can you think of that speak to the goal of reconciliation? (Example: 2 Corinthians 5:18-21)

In Galatians 6, how do you reconcile verse 5 with verse 2?

Can you give an example of how this works?

What does verse 6 mean?

Who do you know that lives out verses 9-10?

How do they emulate the value of not becoming weary of doing good?

Discuss a picture of biblical community. If you can, incorporate scriptural support.

Getting out of the hole:
Invest in being part of the Body of Christ and strengthening the E3 community by increasing the relational risk in your life. Take time to listen to people. Share more of your story. Get more involved by serving alongside fellow E3ers.

Pathways: AXIS

week 04 - connexity

I've always been the girl that knows everyone -- people from every walk of life and every corner of the world. Consequently, it seems as though I've always had (give or take) a bazillion friends. However, in my late teens and early twenties, life threw a cluster of troubled times my way, and I discovered that the number of friends I had was significantly smaller than I thought. I didn't have a bazillion friends. I had two (and apparently a slew of irrelevant surface-level relationships).

Awash in a sea of heartbreak, I held onto this passage in Ecclesiastes like a lifeline. With each tearful sleepover, heart-wrenching phone call, and desperate text, my best friends and I wove together an unbreakable rope I could use to climb out of the dark pit of despair into which I had fallen.

Why these two? They were the only people on the planet I had ever let myself be real with. They were the only ones I ever let see me cry. They were the only ones who knew my struggles, my failures, my faults.

The truth is that God is a raw, relational God. He seeks real, honest relationships with us. Since He created us in His image, we're designed to interact with each other the same way. He didn't create us to carelessly maintain vapid, shallow relationships. He created us to be real with each other. To weep together. To rejoice together. To actually do life together.

Do your relationships mirror God's relationships, or do they emulate something else less fulfilling? Pray on these things. Thank God for his unending grace, and ask Him to help you draw near to your brothers and sisters they way He created you to.

Lindsay Durrenberger spends most of her time ministering to junior high students and trying to change the world's narrow beauty standards via http://fueledbydietcoke.wordpress.com. She also got early access to J.K. Rowling's Pottermore, which makes her super cool and not at all nerdy.

Pathways: AXIS

Journal your thoughts/response here:

Write words or themes you need to meditate on today. Schedule four 5-minute time periods to focus on these things.

day 22 - connexity

I had the privilege of going on a mission trip to Russia – ten days set aside to just work for the Lord. Saturated in prayer, preparations were made. Each day, each appointment, each person was an opportunity to touch a life. We went with hearts motivated to give selflessly and tirelessly, making the time count. It was humbling to be so well received and honored when we had come only to serve in the orphanages, prisons, old folks' homes and on the streets.

That experience changed my life forever. I wanted to live my whole life with that kind of dedication and purpose in my heart to really see people and touch lives, whoever God might put in my path. I learned to plan extra time into my day so I could listen to the hurting, encourage the struggling, and give hope to those on the brink of despair.

The more I pray and seek to love others, the more people come into my life. Just as a fragrant flower releases its scent on to the breeze, I pray that my life would be a "pleasing aroma" that draws others in so they can experience Christ's love through me. It is easy to walk through life caring only for our sphere of responsibility, but Christ's sacrificial example beckons us to hear His heart and follow if we dare.

Carol Meyer Davey finds joy in all things creative and expresses herself in watercolor painting, writing, playing her saxophone and ballroom dancing. She is dedicated to her family and loves being "Grammy" to eight grandchildren.

Pathways: AXIS

Journal your thoughts/response here:

Write words or themes you need to meditate on today. Schedule four 5-minute time periods to focus on these things.

day 23 - connexity

Now you have every spiritual gift you need as you eagerly wait for the return of our Lord Jesus Christ. I Corinthians 1:7

Shouldn't I know what all these spiritual gifts are? But no, I just have a vague recollection and scurry to not only read about them, but worse, find out exactly where they are described. Oh sure, I was tempted to just jump to Romans 12:3-13 or I Corinthians 12:1-31 and omit these first three sentences. Doing so, however, would be an act of pride; the very opposite of what is needed in acknowledging spiritual gifts. Instead, I just feel humbled. It is this kind of reminder that keeps me going as a Christ follower... indeed, my journey started with such humility.

I came to Christ when my life was brought to a complete standstill. As I lay unconscious, aware only of the dark that enveloped me, I heard someone say, "We have some strong medicine for you, but it could kill you. Do you want it?" I could no longer speak, but I grunted anyway. Then, lying paralyzed in the ER, I felt the greatest love of my life. I soared with joy knowing that every hair on my head had been counted. It was the happiest time in my life. I had been humbled to the point where I was totally helpless and could do nothing without help, yet I glowed with joy. Mysterious indeed.

To understand this verse requires humility. I acknowledge that it is not of my own power that I type these words, and doing so reminds me of my desperate need for each and every one of you. Your spiritual gifts make me more complete, and remembering this keeps me appropriately humble. I have the capacity for infinite self-deception; it is only with each other's help that we can form a more perfect union with Christ. Let our spiritual gifts always flourish in E3. This is what happened a few weeks ago when my Growth Group held its meeting at my wife's bedside in the hospital. I pray that we remember to minister to each other in times of strength, as well as weakness, always being humble and knowing that it is not through our own power that we do so.

Frank Fincham is married to Susan (32 years). They have been blessed with 3 wonderful children, Alex (25), Camilla (22), and Jessy (16). Frank has tried to be obedient in describing the miracle of his healing at www.testaments.cjb.net.

Pathways: AXIS

Journal your thoughts/response here:

Write words or
themes you need to
meditate on today. Schedule
four 5-minute time periods to
focus on these things.

day 24 - connexity

God created us for community, for relationship—with Him and with others. He knows that alone, we are more vulnerable. When Jesus was on earth, He even practiced this. He surrounded Himself with His close friends who would walk through life with Him, encourage Him, and pray with Him (unless they fell asleep...but we won't go there). Ecclesiastes 4:12 reminds us that "A person standing alone can be attacked and defeated, but two can stand back-to-back and conquer. Three are even better, for a triple-braided cord is not easily broken." This verse always reminds me of the part in the movie 300 where there are just a few of them and what looks like millions of Persians coming towards them. They pair off in groups and fight back-to-back. Even though it's a little gory, I love it, because it is like watching a living piece of art—each person moving perfectly with the other so that they are continually defending themselves as well as their brothers.

This is what we need to be doing in our community—getting to know each other, working together, "fighting" (think praying) together so much that when the time comes for spiritual battle, we are like a living art piece—working side by side, and praying with and for each other. In that way, we will be able to fight off the attacks of the enemy. I like the analogy of prayer being like fighting a battle because of Ephesians 6, which reminds us that our battle is not against flesh and blood enemies but is a spiritual battle. Community is a beautiful gift from God. He has given us the blessing and the resource of having each other to do life with. He wants us to use the resource He has provided by truly loving each other and doing life together so much that we are ready for the trials when they come. I think that Jars of Clay summed it up well in their song "Shelter":

"If there is any peace, if there is any hope
We must all believe, our lives are not our own
We all belong
God has given us each other
And we will never walk alone."

Rebekah Abbott is half done with nursing school and, in all of her "spare time," she enjoys going to the beach and spending time with her friends and her amazing church family.

Pathways: AXIS

Journal your thoughts/response here:

Write words or
themes you need to
meditate on today. Schedule
four 5-minute time periods to
focus on these things.

day 25 - connexity

Businessdictionary.com defines Connexity as: Interdependence and interrelationship between and among individuals, machines and the global communications network.

As I read the scripture and the definition above, it occurred to me that people have a fantastic ability to communicate. One cannot carry out the statements above while walking around with their head dragging in the sand. In order for these statements to be spoken or experienced, someone had to make an investment in getting to know someone else. Someone had to make an intentional effort to lay aside personal time, to lend a hand, to offer their wares, and to listen when their neighbor was in need. Interdependence with each other involves giving up independence of self. Connexity is the ability to invest in people's lives where they are.

It is said that people don't care what you know until they know that you care. When a neighbor is in crisis, the last thing they need is some bible-thumper condemning them for their part. Advice is better swallowed when there is a relationship that allows for it. A friendly smile, a comforting hug, a meal prepared, a simple nod of reassurance is the knowing, the hearing and the nudge that Jesus spoke about. Engaging in conversations, invitations into your daily routine, and saying yes to an invitation from someone else are ways to practice Connexity. The global communications network, comprised of phones, data texting and the internet, has multiplied the ways we can communicate, giving interrelationships among and between each other new ways to reach people and to strengthen spiritual growth. Building good relationships requires tearing away obstacles and old ways of thought. It is the willingness to be transparent, thus stepping from behind walls of resentment and rejection. It is being gentle with relational boundaries. It is Connexity.

Jeremy Shaw is often seen in the company of his girlfriend Holly, enjoying the outdoors, snapping pictures, or talking to someone who was a stranger five minutes ago.

Pathways: AXIS

Journal your thoughts/response here:

Write words or themes you need to meditate on today. Schedule four 5-minute time periods to focus on these things.

day 26 - connexity

"Spiritual gifts" is difficult terrain to navigate. Often a conversation about this has the potential to end with people feeling discouraged because they aren't doing the things they read about in the Word: healing, performing miracles, and speaking in tongues.

As I'm becoming more of who I believe God has created me to be, I'm finding that the things I've been gifted with don't necessarily fit into the "church" box. Things like "singing pretty" or "enjoying learning people's stories" seem to be inadequate when measured against ones like "prophesy." Gifts come in all shapes and sizes, and scripture says, "A spiritual gift is given to each of us so we can help each other."

So it's not about assessing our gifts and comparing them to the next guy's? We're supposed to help each other? As a broken, wounded soul, I'm not sure that I have the capacity to help people. I don't know what they need, and even if I did, I surely don't know how to help them! What I can do though, is avail myself to God and let Him use my heart, my talents, and abilities as a conduit—to connect people to each other and to Him.

I sing with a band, and once someone carelessly threw away my makeup before a concert. A hair stylist friend offered to do my hair and makeup. In her eyes, she was giving me a gift of her time and abilities. In my eyes, God was speaking, "Sarah, remember that you are Mine. You are loved and valued—even the things that seem insignificant, I see and care about." I cried so much the makeup smeared all over my face.

I'm no Biblical scholar, but I'm confident that "doing hair," and "singing pretty," are not listed in the spiritual gifts' section. You never know how your talent, ability, or the natural tendencies God has imbued you with, might be a vital part of His ministry.

Sarah Mac is a member of the Sarah Mac Band, likes to eat chocolate, and plans to read 52 books before the end of the calendar year.

Pathways: AXIS

Journal your thoughts/response here:

Write words or
themes you need to
meditate on today. Schedule
four 5-minute time periods to
focus on these things.

day 27 - connexity

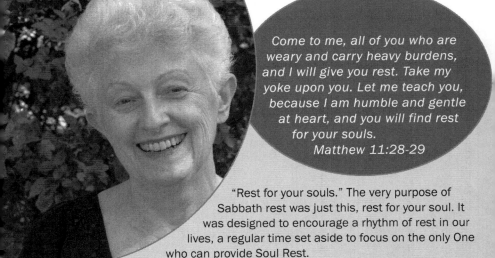

Come to me, all of you who are weary and carry heavy burdens, and I will give you rest. Take my yoke upon you. Let me teach you, because I am humble and gentle at heart, and you will find rest for your souls.
Matthew 11:28-29

"Rest for your souls." The very purpose of Sabbath rest was just this, rest for your soul. It was designed to encourage a rhythm of rest in our lives, a regular time set aside to focus on the only One who can provide Soul Rest.

"Rest for your souls." I've found that Soul Rest cannot co-exist with worry or anxiety. I am compelled to give up my fretting into the hands of Jesus. How can He give rest if I stubbornly cling to my concerns, as if He weren't even there? Pretending He doesn't know? Acting as though He is heedless of my state? Why would He ask me to give up a load that He will not take?

"Take my yoke." The yoke is a device designed to share the burden between two. It means I do not bear the burden alone. Wait! Actually, He says I am to take His yoke. What has happened here? I can only have one yoke, so now, my burden has been replaced by the load He has designed for me. Read one more verse... "For my yoke is easy and my burden is light." That can only mean one thing... this is a win-win situation for me. He gets the heavy stuff and I get Soul Rest!

"I am gentle and humble in heart." That's why He makes the offer. His tender heart sees my back bent beneath a load of care, and He desires to lift it from me. Hands outstretched, He is waiting to exchange heavy for light, stress for peace, chaos for calm.

There were those who tried to tie the Sabbath into a knot of rules and legality, hardly a refreshing day of Soul Rest. Just a few verses later He told them, "... the Son of Man is Lord of the Sabbath."

The Lord of the Sabbath is offering you rest for your soul.

Amy Gwartney is a wife, mother and grandma, and is grateful for each blessing.

Pathways: AXIS

Journal your thoughts/response here:

Write words or
themes you need to
meditate on today. Schedule
four 5-minute time periods to
focus on these things.

day 28 - sabbath

GOING DEEPER

Join the community and go deeper with this Bible study.

Breaking Ground:

Recall a time, when you received the wrong information and acted on it. What happened? When did you realize you did not have it right? How did you respond?

The Dig:

Read Titus 2:1-15.

In verses 1-8, Paul paints a picture of a church where we are to be examples to our community. Who do you see living as an example that you would like to follow?

What are some ways E3 is doing this well? What are some ways that we could improve? Make two lists in your journal section. On the left a "Does Well" column and on the right a "Could Do Better" column.

What could you do, to help our church move the three right column items over to the left

How important do you feel it is, to live a consistent life - at work, home and at play - that is in harmony with your stated beliefs?

In verses 9-10, Paul writes about what should be our attitude and actions while working for someone else. If all Christians adopted an attitude and work ethic that was pleasing to God how would the American workplace be transformed? Economically? Socially? Spiritually?

How would your workplace be transformed if you lived this out?

In verses 11-15, we are instructed "To Make, Mature and Mobilize fully devoted followers of Christ." How are you fulfilling that instruction from God?

Getting out of the hole:

Take some time and do an honest assessment of your contribution to forwarding the Kingdom of Christ. Look at the "Could Do Better" column and make a plan, of how you can become intimately involved in making our church more effective.

Pathways: AXIS

Journal your thoughts/response here:

UPCOMING EVENTS

- **Board Game Night 6PM on 10/14**

- **Pathways Frenchtown Service Project 10/15**

week 05 - discipleship

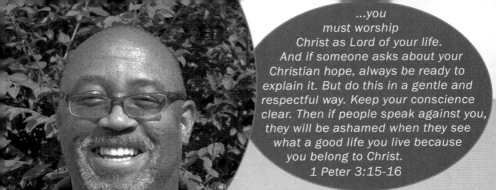

...you must worship Christ as Lord of your life. And if someone asks about your Christian hope, always be ready to explain it. But do this in a gentle and respectful way. Keep your conscience clear. Then if people speak against you, they will be ashamed when they see what a good life you live because you belong to Christ.
1 Peter 3:15-16

When people ask a question about Christianity, it is my duty as a disciple to be able to provide an answer, or more correctly, the answer that will demonstrate that I have learned not just what to believe but why I believe. This is the very essence of discipleship. I should not just come to the gatherings on Sunday and then go out and tell people they need to come hear Pastors Mark, Dan or Eric. I have to tell them why it is important to have a personal one-on-one relationship with Jesus Christ, why going to hell is something to be avoided, why I can have a positive outlook in the face of all adversity, and I have to do this with humility and kindness.

So, I study the Bible, I study the teachings of Jesus, and most importantly, I put Jesus first in all aspects of my life (Mark 8:34-38). I follow his teachings (especially since Jesus Himself stated that this was a requirement to be His disciple, John 8:31-32). Further, I take these truths and share them with other believers to make them better in faith. Then I become that light of the world, the beacon that causes people to pause and ask what is it about Robert that makes him strong in the face of adversity, joyous in the face of sadness, and ecstatic in times of happiness. The answer, of course, is Jesus, Jesus, Jesus!

Now when I am called upon to give a defense of the hope I have in Christ, I don't just speak as a licensed minister, I don't speak as a person raised Pentecostal Holiness, instead I speak as one whose life reflects the words he says. In this way, I reach not only non-believers, but believers also. I might also add that it was this same quality shown by the leadership here that made me choose E3 as my church home. Be Blessed!

Robert Walimuminun is an ordained licensed minister who plays a pretty mean bass guitar. He loves Jesus, the Atlanta Falcons, professional Wrestling, and his church family here at E3!

Pathways: AXIS

Journal your thoughts/response here:

Write words or themes you need to meditate on today. Schedule four 5-minute time periods to focus on these things.

day 29 - discipleship

So encourage each other and build each other up, just as you are already doing. 1 Thessalonians 5:11

Life is generally pretty good, well, really, it's excellent. However, recently I have been experiencing a dry season, one filled with disappointment, discouragement, joy and expectation. In fact, I told others that I felt my life was a country song; the only thing missing was no one was run over by a train! You see, I was laid off from a job that I truly enjoyed and felt called to do, the next day my dog died in my arms, I was given an estimate for a new roof if I want my house to be insured, and then to top it off, my computer died. As the days of the calendar are turned and I continue to apply for jobs and learn of former co-workers who have been hired, there are many times I am feeling disappointed, discouraged, joyful and expectant all at the same time. In fact, I have never had so many conflicting emotions at one time.

Working definitions of *Discipleship* include: The intensely personal activities of two or more persons helping each other experience a growing relationship with God; The process of learning about the teachings of another, internalizing them and then acting upon them.

Jesus never told us that life would be pain or stress free; however, as Christians, Jesus called us to disciple others. I now see that during this dry season, I have been doing exactly what we are called to do. One of my spiritual gifts is exhorter, or what I like to call being a cheerleader. I have been able to disciple others through encouragement by discussing His word and reminding each person that God has a wonderful plan for each of us, that He is faithful and that He has our backs. As a result of many of these conversations, I have witnessed how my friends who were experiencing feelings of depression, discouragement, and disappointment had grown in their relationship with God. On the other hand, I am blessed to have friends who disciple to me, which means so much especially during this dry season.

"Christianity without discipleship is always Christianity without Christ."
-Dietrich Bonhoeffer

Jo Anne Richmond has been part of E3 since the beginning, has a passion for dance, loves to travel, and her favorite song is "Imagine."

Pathways: AXIS

Journal your thoughts/response here:

Write words or themes you need to meditate on today. Schedule four 5-minute time periods to focus on these things.

day 30 - discipleship

I've come to understand that the priority in a Christian's life is to seek, find, and follow the will of God. However, I have to contend with my flawed personality - I'm seriously afflicted with the checklist mentality. Even when I get past that checklist thing, I get so caught up in finding and wanting to follow, that I miss out on the seeking. Then there's the, "I've found it, but do I really have to do that following stuff?" attitude. I've learned that I have to continually remember, refocus, and redirect my walk with Christ.

Seek: I have to continually go looking for God's will. I need to remember that I have to actively search. It's normally not going to come up to me a tap me on the shoulder. To help, I have a manual of sorts (the Bible), but I just can't read it like I do Terry Pratchett. I have to pray about it, asking for insight from the Holy Spirit. I find that when I read scripture while seeking His will, the Holy Spirit "turns on the light." Sometimes it's the ol' 2x4 upside the head, which seems to work better for me.

Find: All the "Find" moments come when I'm seeking. I have, on occasion, initially missed something, but later on when I've had an opportunity to reflect on the situation or event (when I was in the seeking frame of mind), I was able to see the light (or feel lumber, as the case may be).

Follow: Following is the part where sometimes I want to treat God's will like an a la cart menu, but I can't. Although my response has to be voluntary, it is not optional. Voluntarily following God's will is the ultimate sacrifice, greater than anything I could offer.

The connector in all of this is my relationships with other believers who were also seeking, finding and following God's will. Young, old, just starting out, or well on down the road, doing discipleship with others magnifies and multiplies all that God is. It all comes together to show God's Love, His Goodness, His Mercy, His Compassion and His justice.

Larry Coffee loves his family, movies, reading military history and is still learning how to be a disciple of Jesus.

Pathways: AXIS

Journal your thoughts/response here:

Write words or themes you need to meditate on today. Schedule four 5-minute time periods to focus on these things.

day 31 - discipleship

I recently was given a book by a friend with the remark, "...this is a must read." The book's name is *Radical: Taking Back Your Faith from the American Dream*, and the author is David Platt. The title sounded interesting, so I started to read it. Besides many interesting observations David Platt made regarding Christianity in the United States, one observation got my attention immediately. There are 4.5 billion people in the world who have never heard about Christ. In discussions with friends I heard that this number might be overestimated, but I don't think that is really important. A large number of people have never learned about salvation through Christ.

The question therefore is not how many people exactly have not heard about Christ, the question is what am I going to do about it? Of course, I came up with excuses quickly. Lord, I have two small children, what do you want me to do about it? I can't go in the mission field, as much as I want to. However, the conviction remained, and I had to admit, first of all, that I have not even made an attempt to share the message of salvation with my own family in Germany. I thought my life would be witness enough, and one day they were going to get it. As is turns out, my life did not change to "perfect" after my salvation, and so far no one got it. So I decided the next time I go to Germany, I will share the gospel with two people, because that means that there will be two less people out of the 4.5 billion who have not heard the message of salvation.

None of us can change the world, but we can all commit to small steps, and then one day the number of people who have not heard the message of salvation will be a lot smaller.

Elke Puiatti has a bio that is too long to fit on this page, but she has two beautiful children Francisca and Dante.

Pathways: AXIS

Journal your thoughts/response here:

Write words or themes you need to meditate on today. Schedule four 5-minute time periods to focus on these things.

day 32 - discipleship

This past year, I was laid off at the Department of Corrections where I had been working in the Facilities Department. The State offered me a new job as a GED teacher preparing inmates for re-entry at one of the corrections institutions near Tallahassee. The job is challenging. Many of the inmates are young adults in their 20's and 30's who dropped out of school, became addicted to drugs or alcohol, and then committed crimes to support their habit. They test out at 4th and 6th grade level in reading, writing, and arithmetic. As part of re-entry, the State tries to give inmates near release a high school diploma to prevent recidivism. Our program crams eight years of education into twelve months. To make things just a bit more challenging, the education department has to deal with broken furniture, a temperamental HVAC system, worn out text books, inadequate staffing, sparse supplies, software written in DOS, and Intel 386 computers!

As an instructor, I cannot proselytize, but I can encourage. I assign inmates essays and grade them to teach English skills. Some of the topics I assign are: What would my life be like if I believed God loved me? What do I want to do after I get out of prison? How do I find a job or start a small business? How can I love those around me? (e.g. be a good husband, father, or son). On Fridays, students participate in a twenty minute ethics class, during which a wide variety of subjects are discussed, often with a lot of laughter.

Many of the inmates are severely depressed and see themselves as lost. When appropriate, I counsel inmates one on one – stressing that I believe in them, that they are children of God with great talent, and that the Almighty will do great things in their lives - if they ask for Jesus' guidance and grace. When asked, I suggest attending chapel, personal prayer, confession of sin, seeking forgiveness, and reading scripture. Please remember Florida's inmates in your prayers.

Mark Soroko has two grown children and enjoys scuba diving.

Pathways: AXIS

Journal your thoughts/response here:

Write words or
themes you need to
meditate on today. Schedule
four 5-minute time periods to
focus on these things.

day 33 - discipleship

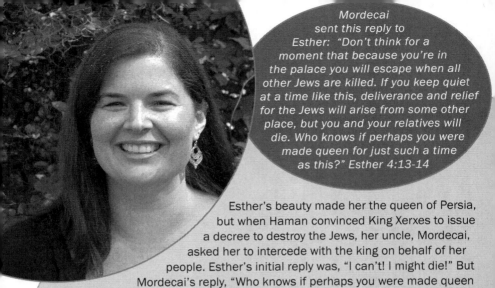

Mordecai sent this reply to Esther: *"Don't think for a moment that because you're in the palace you will escape when all other Jews are killed. If you keep quiet at a time like this, deliverance and relief for the Jews will arise from some other place, but you and your relatives will die. Who knows if perhaps you were made queen for just such a time as this?"* Esther 4:13-14

Esther's beauty made her the queen of Persia, but when Haman convinced King Xerxes to issue a decree to destroy the Jews, her uncle, Mordecai, asked her to intercede with the king on behalf of her people. Esther's initial reply was, "I can't! I might die!" But Mordecai's reply, "Who knows if perhaps you were made queen for just such a time as this?" convinced her otherwise.

All too often, I find myself reacting to challenges much in the same way that Esther did. Although my challenges never involve the fate of an entire people, my fear of failure, confrontation, or just a new experience still cause my first thought to be, "Wait! I can't do that!" Recently, I realized that I am doing myself a great disservice by automatically assuming I will fail. Maybe I face new challenges for a reason. Maybe God puts me in certain times and places because I have a particular skill, a certain experience, or an ability that makes me the right person for the job.

We are given opportunities everyday to fulfill God's will. It may be as simple as lending someone your cell phone to call a tow truck, or it may be something complicated, like speaking into someone's life about addiction. It may be an unexpected promotion or a chance to get involved in the community. Initially, we may feel ill-equipped to meet whatever challenge we face and assume that we don't have the internal or external resources to do so. But God chooses us specifically for our challenges, and all of our experiences, good or bad, have prepared us for them. Whatever we face may be difficult and frightening, but it is a chance to serve God and grow as individuals, and sometimes the best thing we can do is trust that God has made us for just such a time as this.

Christy Tucker enjoys movies, stripey socks, and dead languages. She is proudly owned by her cat, Gracie.

Pathways: AXIS

Journal your thoughts/response here:

Write words or themes you need to meditate on today. Schedule four 5-minute time periods to focus on these things.

day 34 - discipleship

"Go out and stand before me on the mountain," the Lord told him. And as Elijah stood there, the Lord passed by, and a mighty windstorm hit the mountain... but the Lord was not in the wind. ...the Lord was not in the earthquake. ...the Lord was not in the fire. And after the fire there was the sound of a gentle whisper. When Elijah heard it, he wrapped his face in his cloak and went out and stood at the entrance of the cave. 1 Kings 19:11-13

In this verse, God does something that baffles me. He can present Himself to Elijah in any way He likes, and He chooses a *whisper* of all things. The thing about whispers is that you have to listen for them. In a crowded room you would notice an earthquake or tornado, but you would miss a whisper unless you were listening.

At the beginning of the chapter, Elijah spends 40 days running away from people who are trying to kill him. At the end of this marathon, he finds the cave where he hears God speak, which I think is important. There is nothing wrong with the time Elijah spends running, but at some point he has to stop and slow down to hear God's whisper. Listening is a skill that is hard to practice while running.

I guess what I am trying to get at is that I think God wants to whisper to us. I think I miss moments where He wants to whisper to me when I don't make rest a priority in my life—when I am too busy to stop moving for a moment. Not saying I always have the opportunity to physically stop —it looks different each day—but there is some moment where I can rest and listen. In the words of the poet Elizabeth Barrett Browning, "Earth's crammed with Heaven, and every common bush afire with God; but only he who sees, takes off his shoes."

Cody Fox recently moved to Thomasville and married the love of his life, Katie Hanna. He is currently a graduate student at Valdosta, studying to become a teacher. He enjoys writing poetry and playing music in his free time.

Pathways: AXIS

Journal your thoughts/response here:

Write words or themes you need to meditate on today. Schedule four 5-minute time periods to focus on these things.

day 35 - sabbath

GOING DEEPER

Join the community and go deeper with this Bible study.

Breaking Ground:

Who do you admire more: a person who works hard and fails, or a person who succeeds without much effort?

The Dig:

Read Matthew 25:14-30.

What skills are you known for?

Do you use those skills on a regular basis or do they lay dormant?

What do you think is the point of this story that Jesus is trying to convey?

Who does the master represent? The journey? The money? The servants?

Why do you think the servants get different amounts of money? What is Jesus trying to convey?

Who do you know that seems to have a big entrustment of talents?

Have you ever witnessed someone who has been entrusted with a lot of talent and let it go to waste?

What about the opposite? Have you ever seen a person who does not have a lot of talent, but they worked hard and succeed?

What do you think would have happened if the servant who buried the money had tried their best to invest it, but failed?

What does this parable teach us about how God views the talent He has entrusted to us?

Getting out of the hole:

Get involved! Find a place to help forward God's kingdom. If you don't know your "talents" then plan to take the Stage Class, Demonstrate, in November

Pathways: AXIS

Journal your thoughts/response here:

UPCOMING EVENTS

- E3's Rock-N-Roll
  Costume Ball
  7PM on 10/28

- Serve Tallahassee
  9AM on 10/29

week 06 - service

I believe service is a scary word for some followers of Christ. This lost and hurting world can be overwhelming, and we find ourselves wondering where to start. God has been teaching me through my experiences that having a heart for service comes through obedience (another scary word, I know).

In Luke22, Jesus tells his disciples to take the lowest rank. Get started by taking on things in your community that, quite frankly, no one wants to do. It may be something small, perhaps even unnoticed to most, but not to God. You'll find yourself fulfilled in a new way because of your service to others and to God.

Jesus also tells us that ordinarily the master sits at the table and is served. How do I get that seat? According to Jesus, that's not my seat; it's not even His seat, for He is our servant! Grasping this concept has drastically changed my outlook on service.

I'd being lying if I said that service is something I'm always excited about. Here's where the obedience comes in. What happens when we use our time, money, and energy to meet the needs of others? We become more like Jesus. Jesus says He is our servant, so as we are serving others, He is serving us! God knows our needs better than we do. We just have to learn to trust Him and take comfort in the knowledge that He is our provider.

When we start saying yes to opportunities to serve, our hearts grow closer to God. Our mindset begins to transform, and we become more and more eager to show love to one another. What a beautiful thing! My heart breaks for children, families, the underprivileged, and so many other things. Knowing my selfish nature, if my heart is broken for these things, it's God doing the heartbreaking. What better for a broken heart than love?

Show love by serving someone today and experience the joy of allowing Jesus to serve you!

Elizabeth Wilkes is just a gal learning to follow a guy named Jesus.

Pathways: AXIS

Journal your thoughts/response here:

Write words or themes you need to meditate on today. Schedule four 5-minute time periods to focus on these things.

day 36 - service

This is a weird verse for me... one I feel challenged to write on. It's very easy to expound on how everyone has gifts from God and how they can all be used to His glory in service. True, but it's not the whole truth.

The word for gift in this verse is *charisma,* the scholarly understanding of which is 'gift of grace.' These gifts are granted to us by God, through His grace, so they come with a responsibility. We must use them wisely and to serve others. By doing so we fulfill the second half of the verse and become the faithful stewards we are supposed to be. It isn't just that we are able to serve others with our gifts, our charisma; it's that if we want to be faithful to God's grace, we need to serve others with them.

I said that I feel a challenge to write on this verse. That challenge comes from making sure in doing so I'm not being a hypocrite. I very recently stopped pursuing a career in theatre to pursue one in nursing. I have laid aside an artistic gifting, at least professionally, for a more directly "service-related" career field. So, I need to be certain that I am not forsaking the gifts God has given me by seeking out a way to serve others that is contrary to His plan for me. I would still be a poor steward of my gifts if I attempted to serve people in a way I'm not equipped for.

So what is the whole truth? Well, probably more than I've said here, but at least some of it is that to be a faithful steward, we must understand what our gifts are, use them to serve others, and in our service, make sure we are not forsaking the gifts God has given us. In wrestling with this verse, I was able to understand that my new career will simply utilize other gifts God has granted me, and it doesn't preclude me from continuing to utilize my artistic ones in service.

Lane Forsman is a Tallahassee native who recently returned from three years with AmeriCorps to pursue a degree in nursing. Green is his favorite color.

Pathways: AXIS

Journal your thoughts/response here:

Write words or themes you need to meditate on today. Schedule four 5-minute time periods to focus on these things.

day 37 - service

When I first started supervising people, I was clueless. I didn't read any books or attend any motivational workshops. I was just thrown into the fire (a team of people with children my age). I was too busy to reflect on my leadership style at the time, but then I began my study of educational leadership. There are many models of leadership out there. Transformational Leadership seems to be the trendiest. Even the name sounds cool, right? Who wouldn't want to be transformed? But, when you look deeper, a follower discovers that he/she is being transformed into what the leader has in mind. Knowing some of the leaders I've seen and worked with – that doesn't sound very appealing. As a leader, I find that doesn't sound very appealing either – I don't really want to be manipulating people to get them to do what I want.

As I studied, I came across another model called Servant Leadership. The more I read about it, the more I recognized that it is the way Jesus leads me and how I naturally lead others. Jesus didn't give grand motivational speeches for thousands of people at a time night after night. He washed his disciples' feet. He didn't try to work his way up in the Jewish religious hierarchy. He healed the sick. He didn't work 18-hour days so he could move up the organizational ladder just a little more. He wept with those who mourned.

We are all leaders in some capacity. We all lead others by our example, whether they are our co-workers, people we supervise, students in a classroom, or our families. Although I naturally tend toward Servant Leadership, if I'm honest with myself, I recognize that I'm not always willing to do the dirty work, take time out of my busy schedule to call someone who is ill, or be vulnerable enough to allow my heart to be broken for others. I believe that God has given me the gift of leadership. What I don't know is what that will look like in the future. As I wait for His plan to unfold, I am grateful for Jesus' model as a guide.

Theresa Bogema harbors the secret desire to eat out of the peanut butter jar with a Hershey bar.

Pathways: AXIS

Journal your thoughts/response here:

Write words or themes you need to meditate on today. Schedule four 5-minute time periods to focus on these things.

day 38 - service

Division of Labor + Spirit Led = Wisdom and Rest - Producing a healthy church and community.

I have been a commercial cleaner for a good part of my working adulthood. Through work experience and trial and error, I have expanded my knowledge on how to effectively clean things such as carpets and windows, and how to strip and wax hardwood floors. While I am quite capable of doing other things, this is one type of job that fits me very well as I have always enjoyed the physical work.

God led me to E3 and, almost immediately, I wanted to volunteer to clean. I found out that they were actually paying a commercial cleaning company. I told them to fire that cleaning company, and I would take over and make sure it got done; of course, I could not do it myself, so I volunteered to lead.

Over the years I have volunteered for "Serve Tallahassee" and been a leader of Growth Groups; it became too much. I began taking on a "Martha" attitude sometimes... looking at others to pitch in and resenting them almost for not jumping in! At the same time, when others who had jumped in and had no clue how cleaning worked, it was so comical that I had to go hide so they would not see me laughing. I was wrong and God had to show me that I had to put my time in serving Him into one thing and one thing only, making sure that E3 is ready for Sunday guests.

I may never go to Guatemala, Benin, or any other mission trip. I will never be on stage singing or playing an instrument (I have no desire to do so, and besides, I do not like the idea of rotten tomatoes being thrown at me). I will never stand and give a sermon. However, when I do serve God by cleaning E3, I am enabling people to move on God's behalf and this knowledge makes me extremely happy.

Kim Goodner has been a commercial cleaner for the past 15 years. She is also the proud mother of two grown children: April and Aaron.

Pathways: AXIS

Journal your thoughts/response here:

Write words or
themes you need to
meditate on today. Schedule
four 5-minute time periods to
focus on these things.

day 39 - service

A few years ago I served as chair of the board of a group home for children. During my tenure, our CEO misused $500,000 of trust funds for general operating expenses without our board's knowledge, creating a liability and a discredit to our organization. As a result, we lost the support of major donors and others. The national organization holding our charter and land rights threatened to shut us down and requested removal of the board.

Our board had served faithfully and acted diligently in finding the improper use of funds and acted quickly to form a recovery plan. Our actions as a group included prayer and faith in knowing that God would provide for us, and that we could work hard to overcome our crisis. Our work showed our faith and convinced others to use our board to reorganize and overcome the challenge, despite the existing protocol that our board should be held responsible and replaced. It would have been easy to step down and expect God to do his work through others; however, we knew that God had equipped our board for this challenge, and stepping aside voluntarily would not be for the best.

The next two years God was faithful to meet every need. People came forward to serve in critical roles, and God provided large financial gifts from unexpected sources with amazing timing. Through hard work and planning, combined with faith in God's grace and provision, the group home was able to eliminate over $750,000 in debt, becoming debt free for the first time in many years. Monthly financial stability was established through hiring a well-qualified director and re-gearing its services.

Through our group's service during a difficult time, we had faith in God. Having faith required us to continue in service, demonstrating that faith, coupled with good deeds, will be seen by others. Today this group home continues to serve broken families and children and has regained the trust of past donors whose funds were misused. God uses experience of all types. I believe through this service God has prepared me for another need.

Brian and Vicki Bellamy live in Thomasville, GA. Brian is an attorney, and Vicki is a mother of 5 children ages 13 and under.

Pathways: AXIS

Journal your thoughts/response here:

Write words or themes you need to meditate on today. Schedule four 5-minute time periods to focus on these things.

day 40 - service

God in the final judgment tells us what we do for others we do for Him. Service seems to come naturally to some of us; it does for me. This summer I was in Wisconsin away from my service positions. I was incredibly blessed by my friends and family. Day in and out, meals were made, food provided, clothes washed, a car was lent to me, and we were on the guest list to all the attractions. I was being served! Instead of seeing Jesus in those I serve, I was watching Him in those who served me.

The Bible says, "Worship and serve Him with your whole heart and a willing mind. For the Lord sees every heart and knows every plan and thought. If you seek him, you will find Him." 1 Chronicles 28:9b. I seek God and I find Him in everyone around me. I was able to serve in different ways as God lead, even on vacation. I found that when I was willing to serve in other ways than I was comfortable with, God was able to use me in many ways.

Service is exactly what keeps us moving as the Body of Christ. Each of us is vital to the health of our community. As being the beloved of God, we have the opportunity to notice the ways we are the Body. We have the privilege to serve God and to see Him in each other; the opportunity to be the tangible hands of Christ. The right heart-posture, a willingness to serve, and a love for God is a great place to begin to do His work. I also want to encourage having accountability in making the right choices with your service. You're never alone; God will provide all you need to do His work. "I thank Christ Jesus our Lord, who has given me strength to do his work. He considered me trustworthy and appointed me to serve him." 1 Timothy 1:12

You're gonna have to serve somebody, it may be the devil or it may be the Lord, but you're gonna have to serve somebody. -Bob Dylan, 1979

Paula Kapral is the mother of Christian, Nicholaus and Hachi. She is not perfect but she is forgiven.

Pathways: AXIS

Journal your thoughts/response here:

Write words or
themes you need to
meditate on today. Schedule
four 5-minute time periods to
focus on these things.

day 41 - service

In the United States, rest is a weird concept for many to grasp. With a tendency to be motivated by money and greed, many Americans work around the clock to make sure they can afford the latest gadgets and nicest cars. Always wanting more, people become blinded by what society tells us we need to have. On the opposite end of the spectrum are those who don't work hard enough, mooching off of everyone around them. What might come to mind is the 30-year-old couch potato living in his mother's basement. Perhaps the answer lies somewhere in the middle.

In the scripture above, God tells us that the Sabbath day of rest is dedicated to Him. To me, this means that we need to free ourselves from the many distractions of this world and focus solely on Him; praising Him in all His glory. I believe this verb "rest" is meant in an active sense, as opposed to the inactive vibe it tends to have. Dictionary.com defines rest (noun) as a "mental or spiritual calm; tranquility" which would imply that rest is more about the mental state than the physical condition. I say that because I cannot count the number of times I have heard people say "I can't go to church. God says I'm supposed to stay home and rest."

A few months ago, I decided to take the summer off from volunteering in E3Kids. My plan was to use the time as a sabbatical in a sense, and spend a lot of time in prayer, asking God what ministry He would like me to work with in the fall. I did spend time in prayer, seeking out His will for me; however, when opportunities came up for me to volunteer in other ministries, I immediately declined as they interfered with my time of "rest." While this may have been what God wanted me to do, I somehow think it was my laziness consuming me.

This topic seems to have come up at just the right time for me. Fall is almost here, and I'm ready to serve God in whatever He calls me to do. I hope to carry this new sense of the word "rest" with me from here on out.

Lindsey Newberry is a 24-year-old trying to keep her feet on the path God has for her.

Pathways: AXIS

Journal your thoughts/response here:

Write words or themes you need to meditate on today. Schedule four 5-minute time periods to focus on these things.

day 42 - sabbath

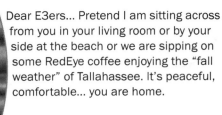

Dear E3ers... Pretend I am sitting across from you in your living room or by your side at the beach or we are sipping on some RedEye coffee enjoying the "fall weather" of Tallahassee. It's peaceful, comfortable... you are home.

Then I ask a simple question, "What do you want out of life?"

The walls close in for some of you. Some of you are running from the impending tsunami or have burned lips and are choking on your coffee. Some of you are eerily peaceful because you know God is leading you and you don't have the full answer to that question yet but you know it is coming. Some of you might just smile like you see people do when they are saying goodbye to a job they hated. But the question remains.

We are called to be His. We are called to look out at the vast ocean of possibilities and follow Him through the maze of options. Each step of the way He is with us. There is no place we go that He is absent. But the steps are ours... yours and mine. We take them with strength earned and strength given. We point the way and head out to find purpose because God has more.

I pray that you have found purpose in these last 40 days - that you have found reason and truth to stir worship for the living God that flows from every part of your being. I pray that you have seen bad habits broken and good habits formed and I pray that you stay the course. I pray that you have gained energy by spending energy in community and that you have seen and confirmed in your heart that God is deeply in love with you so that you might continue to be healed by His grace.

At E3, we would seek to equip you and encourage you on the journey to be a "fully devoted follower of Christ." We facilitate Growth Groups and offer worship gatherings and provide Stage Classes so that you might be drawn deeper into fellowship with God and His Body. We can only facilitate Pathways for you to walk on but the walk is yours. You must own the vision.

Press on in this journey and you will see the glory of God. Persevere in this path and you will experience more of His life-changing love that will transform your mind and heart and empower you to offer that hope to others. Press on and press in for the King is worthy of your best efforts and desires unhindered relationship with you.

For the glory of Jesus,
Pastor Dan Meyer